Live online learning
A facilitator's guide

ISBN: 978-1-4475-0004-9

First published in 2011

http://morethanblended.com/

Live online learning
A facilitator's guide

Contents

Whys and wherefores	4
Planning your session	12
Communicating with voice and live video	20
Communicating using images and text	26
Sharing resources	34
Building in interactivity	38
Building up to the session	46
Facilitating the session	52
Following up	58

MORE THAN
BLENDED LEARNING

1

Whys and wherefores

1

Whys and wherefores

What it means to be live and online

Before we get started, let's just clarify our terms of reference. To do this, we will have to introduce some words - 'synchronous' and 'asynchronous' - that you wouldn't normally use in polite company; we are not doing this for effect, nor do we intend to use terminology like this throughout this guide. It's just that these are the correct words for the job and are commonly used in e-learning, so you may as well add them to your vocabulary.

Synchronous communication requires all participants to make themselves available at an agreed time. It's live and it's real-time. It can be contrasted with asynchronous communication, which frees up participants from the need to be available at the same time. Asynchronous communication is self-paced; you have as long as you like to reflect on what others have to say and how you want to respond.

Here are some examples:

Synchronous communication	Asynchronous communication
Face-to-face comms	Letters
Telephone	Printed materials
Chat rooms	Tapes, CDs
Video conferencing	Email, blogs, forums
Instant messaging	Web content
Web conferencing	Self-paced e-learning

To be 'online' implies a state of connectivity, typically through a device such as a computer that is connected to the internet or an organisation's intranet. Face-to-face communication is clearly not online. Most traditional media, including print publications, tapes, CDs, radio and TV can be regarded as offline media.

Just to be clear, live online communication occurs in real-time over a computer network such as the internet. That's the only type of communication we're concerned with here.

Tools for live online communication

Instant messaging (IM) is the most common form of live online communication. Typically there are just two people involved, but the technology will support larger numbers. Originally IM was based on simple text messaging, but now usually involves both online audio and video. Programs include Windows Live Messenger, Yahoo Messenger, Google Talk, IBM Lotus Sametime and Skype. IM was originally the preserve of PC and Macintosh users, but is now also widely available on mobile devices.

Web conferencing is used to conduct live meetings, training sessions, briefings or presentations via the internet. The extended functionality of web conferencing systems usually requires participants to

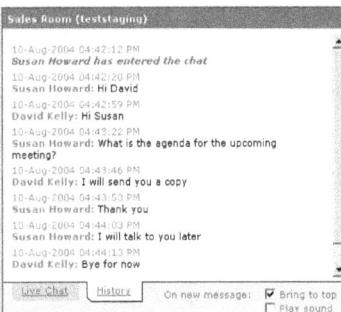

Tools for live online communication range from simple chat rooms through to high-end video conferencing

download a special client application to their computers. This functionality includes online audio and video, application sharing, electronic whiteboards, shared media (such as PowerPoint presentations), text chat and polling. Most systems will also support voice communication using teleconferencing for those participants who don't have the hardware or the bandwidth to support online audio. Web conferencing systems include Cisco WebEx, Microsoft LiveMeeting, Saba Centra, Citrix GoToMeeting, Adobe Acrobat Connect, Elluminate and DimDim.

Video conferencing uses digital telecommunications to support remote meetings that employ both audio and video. The boundary between what can be achieved with video conferencing and with simpler instant messaging and web conferencing systems is increasingly blurred, although high end 'telepresence' systems, that provide a highly authentic, high-definition interface are still very much at the top end.

There are many tools that support live online communication. In this guide we're concentrating on web conferencing, which is the type of tool you're most likely to use for learning and development.

The three main applications for web conferencing

1. A webinar is an online seminar/lecture/presentation, delivered using web conferencing software. Webinars are good for sharing ideas and experiences, much like any typical session at a face-to-face conference.

2. A web meeting enables participants to provide each other with updates, solve problems and make decisions, just like a regular meeting.

3. A live online learning event (or 'virtual classroom' as it's often called) uses web conferencing software to facilitate learning. Of course you could also learn something from a webinar or online meeting, but in the virtual classroom learning is the explicit purpose.

	Webinar	*Web meeting*	*Virtual classroom*
Primary purpose	To share ideas and experiences	To solve problems and make decisions	To facilitate learning
Face-to-face equivalent	A session at a seminar or conference	A short business meeting	A classroom session
Who's in charge?	The host and/or presenter	The chair of the meeting	The teacher / trainer
Visual focus	Slides; presenter webcam; text chat; polls; website tours	Participant webcams; shared documents; slides	Slides; whiteboard; questions/polls; shared applications; website tours; text chat
Auditory focus	Host / presenters' voices	Participants' voices	Teacher/trainer's voice and participants' voices
Interactive focus	Text chat; polls	Voice	Text chat; whiteboards; polls; voice; application sharing

Webinars, web meetings and virtual classrooms use the same technologies but are quite different in character

This guide could help you to run good webinars or online meetings, but that is not its purpose. The focus here is live online learning in the virtual classroom.

Why learn online?

Learning online is clearly more efficient than getting together face-to-face: it saves a large amount of money that would otherwise have been spent on travel and subsistence, not to mention all the wasted travelling time; learning where you normally work is also more environmentally friendly, which has to be a good thing; it encourages shorter sessions (how many workshops are padded out to last a full day?); and if some element of a session is not directly relevant to you, you can always do something else while you wait.

Generally speaking, if you use the same instructional methods, it doesn't matter too much which medium you use - face-to-face or online you'll get similar results. However, not all methods can be implemented online - sometimes you just have to be face-to-face if you're going to get the job done, and if that's the case, then live online learning will fail.

However, there are also circumstances in which you might get *more* effective results online than you could achieve face-to-face:

• Participants don't need to travel, which means you can arrange a session as soon as the need arises.

• You will find it easier to attract the participation of experts who are geographically distant from you. You may never get a specialist to travel across the world to contribute to your face-to-face event, but they will find it hard to object to making available an hour of their time online.

- Web conferencing allows a degree of anonymity, so introverts may find it easier to contribute than they would face-to-face.

- You can record sessions, so that those who miss a live event can catch up later.

....

As long as learning online doesn't stop you from using the instructional methods that are best suited to the requirement, you'll make big savings in terms of resources and be able to respond more quickly to needs.

....

Why learn in real-time?

As we've seen, communication can be synchronous or asynchronous, and when you design a learning intervention, you have the choice between the two. Given the advantages of being asynchronous - self-pacing, freedom over when you learn and for how long - there has to be a good reason for going synchronous. Here are some arguments for starters:

- When real-time interaction with experts is critical; participants must have questions answered before they can move on.

- When it is important for people to interact and share ideas concurrently.

- When the facilitator must be able to observe that participants have mastered a skill. By engaging in practical exercises in a live event, participants can demonstrate real-time skills and thinking.

When your session is online, you will find it easier to attract the participation of experts who are geographically distant from you.

- When a live event will help to ensure that a learning task is completed. Participants are more likely to carry out a self-paced task, such as reading or writing up an assignment, if they know a live event is coming up at which they will have to report on their progress. Nancy White describes how "synchronous events can provide a heartbeat for an ongoing community, group or network. We put them on our agenda instead of saying 'I'll do that later' and they focus our attention."

- When conveying late-breaking and time-sensitive information.

- When there is a need to adjust the level

When to be synchronous	When to be asynchronous
When real-time interaction with experts is critical.	When participants have very different needs, priorities or preferences.
When it is important for people to interact and share ideas concurrently.	When participants need to research or reflect carefully before making contributions.
When the facilitator must be able to observe that participants have mastered a skill.	When there are participants who find it difficult to make their best contributions in a synchronous environment.
When a live event will help to ensure that a learning task is completed.	
When conveying late-breaking and time-sensitive information.	When it is difficult to arrange synchronous events because participants are based in different time zones or have conflicting obligations and commitments.
When there is a need to adjust the level or complexity of material in real-time based on the way participants are responding to the material.	When participants need to be able to refer to the same materials repeatedly.
When questions and areas of difficulty cannot be easily predicted in advance.	When participants will benefit from the opportunity to learn at any time that suits them.
When there isn't the time or budget to develop asynchronous materials.	When it is advantageous for participants to read/listen/watch at their own pace.
When the presence of a trainer will contribute significantly to learning.	When the learning is best accomplished in small chunks.
When a guest expert has limited time availability.	When the learning needs to be available on demand.

The arguments for synchronous and asynchronous communication are finely balanced, which is why it often pays to combine the two in a blended learning solution

or complexity of material in real-time based on the way participants are responding to the material.

- When questions and areas of difficulty cannot be easily predicted in advance.

- When there isn't the time or budget to develop asynchronous materials, such as some self-paced e-learning.

- When the presence of a trainer will contribute significantly to learning. As Jonathan Finkelstein reports: "People need not be present concurrently with an instructor to simply have information passed on to them, yet the active construction of knowledge by learners through a process of real-time give and take is well served in a live online setting."

- When a guest expert is available for a limited time only and couldn't respond to questions in a forum over a longer period.

When you design a learning intervention, you can choose which elements are live and which are self-paced. Given that self-paced learning is more flexible as far as the learner is concerned, make sure you have good reasons for going live.

When live online learning is not enough

It's probably already occurred to you that, in many cases, a learning intervention will benefit from a mix of synchronous and asynchronous elements: some of which may need to be face-to-face, while others will be more efficiently conducted online. In other words, you need a *blended solution*.

A blend is likely to be the best option when the intervention is lengthy; when there is more than one type of learning to be accomplished (i.e. a mix of knowledge, interpersonal skills, physical skills, problem-solving skills, attitude change); and also in those situations where the target audience is varied in terms of prior learning, interests, motivation and preferences.

A live online learning event can stand alone, but it's just as likely to be part of a blended solution, which could include self-paced activities and perhaps face-to-face events.

2

Planning your session

2

Planning your session

Be clear what you're aiming to achieve

The purpose of a learning intervention can be viewed at three different levels: the organisational aims that the intervention is designed to support, the changes in performance that are required if the aims are to be achieved, and the learning (the knowledge, skills and attitudinal changes) which is required if performance is to change. If these outcomes are not absolutely clear, you really do need to conduct some research before you design the online session, otherwise there is no way you will be able to determine whether an online session is an appropriate response, what you should cover in the session and what instructional methods you should use.

As they say, if you don't know where you're going, any path will lead you there. And we need to be a bit more precise than that.

Select the right strategy to meet the learning requirement

You will find it helpful to distinguish between the different types of learning objectives, because these tend to benefit from different instructional methods:

- Procedural tasks are step-by-step activities completed much the same way each time. These benefit from demonstrations followed by hands-on practice with feedback.

- Principle-based tasks are governed by guidelines that are implemented differently each time. Here participants need to see demonstrations showing how the task is carried out in a variety of situations and then practice the task in diverse situations. These tasks are especially amenable to group settings.

- A process is a series of stages that operate in sequence on a cause and effect basis. Examples of processes include the workings of a computer, the way learning occurs in the brain, or the stages in performance management. You can help people to understand a process using diagrams, experiments, case studies and simulations.

- Facts are arbitrary pieces of information that need to be memorised or referred to as needed. It is not easy to remember facts, so nothing beats repeated practice.

- A concept is a word or phrase that represents a whole class of items that share common features. 'Word processing' is a concept, whereas the product 'Microsoft Word' is a fact; 'actor' is a concept, whereas the name 'Harrison Ford' is a fact. To teach concepts you need to explain the unique characteristics of the concept, provide lots of examples and then have participants identify correct and incorrect examples.

Type of learning	Definition	Strategy
Procedural tasks	Step-by-step activities completed much the same way each time.	Demonstrations followed by hands-on practice with feedback.
Principle-based tasks	Tasks governed by guidelines that are implemented differently each time.	Demonstrations showing how the task is carried out in a variety of situations, followed by practice of the task in diverse situations.
Process	A series of stages that operate in sequence on a cause and effect basis.	Help people to understand a process using diagrams, experiments, case studies and simulations.
Facts	Arbitrary pieces of information that need to be memorised or referred to as needed.	Repeated rehearsal, perhaps with the aid of mnemonics.
Concepts	Words or phrases that represent whole classes or categories of items that share common features.	Explain the unique characteristics of the concept, provide lots of examples and then have participants identify correct and incorrect examples.

Different types of learning require quite different teaching strategies

Most learning topics in the workplace are task based, because your goal is typically to change performance in some way. However, it is often necessary for participants to have an understanding of key underlying facts and concepts in order to carry out the task in question. Usually it's better to teach the facts and concepts first, rather than as you explain the task.

You can increase engagement by converting traditional *didactic teaching* (that's where you present the content, provide examples and then ask questions or have participants practice) into *inductive learning* (where you provide examples, then derive the key learning points by asking challenging questions about the examples, only then moving on to check understanding and having participants practise). The inductive approach is best for teaching principle-based tasks or concepts, but is not suited to teaching facts and procedures, where the learning is much more black and white.

Your role as designer of the session is to select the most appropriate methods and media to meet the particular objectives. Often the best approach is to combine a live online session with asynchronous methods used before and after. It can be helpful to think of the session as a real-time event packaged with preparation and information sharing ahead of time and continued reflection and sharing afterwards.

....

Different types of learning objectives require very different strategies and instructional methods. Make sure you know what type of learning you're aiming at and that your strategies and methods are up to the task.

....

Get to know your audience

If goals are the end point you are aiming towards, then your audience is your starting point. And with adults you are never starting from a point of complete ignorance, regardless of the topic. This is a help not a hindrance, because learning can only occur when learners are able to connect new information to what they already know.

It is important to find out as much as you can about your audience, before you design your session:

It is important to find out as much as you can about your audience, before you design your session

- Of course there are the demographics – age, gender and the suchlike, which might influence your design, depending on the topic.

- Of more significance is likely to be what they already know about the subject in question, what their attitude is to this subject, and what associated skills they currently possess. It matters most when these starting positions vary a great deal from person to person, because this can make it more difficult to work with them in groups and to follow any form of uniform and fixed curriculum. The same problems can be experienced when learners differ substantially in terms of their own objectives (irrespective of what they already know or can do), because of different priorities in their jobs and careers.

- Learners also differ in what psychologists like to call their *metacognitive skills*, their ability to self-direct their own learning.

Some learners are more dependent than others on structure in the learning process; some are quite capable of tackling just about any subject using their own initiative. This matters a great deal, because you simply cannot expect those with poor metacognitive skills to flourish in a free-form, exploratory learning environment. Similarly, independent learners can become frustrated by what they see as the stifling formality and rigid structure imposed by many classroom events and interactive e-learning courses.

- Learners can also differ in terms of their preferences for how they learn. It's important to remember, however, that learners are quite capable of learning in any number of ways, whether or not they prefer the method that's been selected for them. It's also clear that, unless you're sure that the majority of your audience have roughly the same

morethanblended.com

preferences (it doesn't take a genius to know that you'll need to design a different course for accountants than for salespeople), there's not a lot you can do about it except to build as much variety into your course as you can.

- And don't forget the cultural differences. You cannot simply export a learning intervention from one country to another, without knowing about the norms, values and practices of that country and then modifying the intervention accordingly. If you're running an event for a multi-cultural audience, then you'll have to take particular care to ensure you do not ride rough over any important cultural sensitivities.

Your audience is your starting point. The way you design your session will be heavily influenced by what you can find out about their needs, capabilities, interests, preferences and cultural differences.

How many people and for how long?

Just because a web conferencing system may be capable of supporting hundreds of participants at the same time, doesn't mean that this is a good idea. The larger the audience, the less you can respond to the needs of each individual and the less time they get to participate. Webinars are different, because they are modelled on conference sessions where one or more experts dominate the air time, and interaction is limited to Q&A. You probably wouldn't want more participants in a virtual classroom than you would face-to-face; in fact some experts believe that, given the extra burdens on online facilitators, you should aim for no more than 75% of the numbers you would invite to the equivalent face-to-face session.

You would not normally expect an online session to last more than 90 minutes. It's really hard to sustain motivation for much longer than this. Obviously many face-to-face sessions are a lot longer, but then this is as much for logistical reasons as anything else - if classroom sessions were limited to 90 minutes, the ratio of travel time to classroom time would be unacceptable. One of the great benefits of learning online is that shorter sessions really are practical and, what's more, they're much more effective. Participants definitely prefer learning in small chunks and so do their brains.

If you have a lot to cover in a short time, you may not be able to spread your intervention over a period of many days. In this case, make sure you take regular and quite lengthy breaks. You could also try interspersing the live sessions with asynchronous activities - perhaps some individual practice, reading, reflecting and so on.

> "Design a highly-interactive session that takes advantage of the fact that participants are together in real-time."

Limit the number of participants to the numbers you would expect for a face-to-face session, perhaps less. Keep sessions short. If you need to chain a number of sessions together, take regular breaks and consider asyncrhonous activities in between.

Structure the session

The way you structure your session will, of course, depend on the learning strategies and instructional methods you are using. However, you may find some of the following tips useful, particularly for kicking off your session:

- Consider creating an activity for early-arriving participants to complete while they wait for the session to begin. This could be a whiteboard activity, helping them to get used to the markup tools (there's more on whiteboards later if you're not sure what this means). Alternatively, you could develop a Flash movie, a narrated PowerPoint presentation or a video that presents information about the format of the session and the tools you will be using.

- Create an introductory slide that presents the title of the session, the start and finish times, and the facilitator's name and photo. You may precede this with a slide that shows a screen shot of

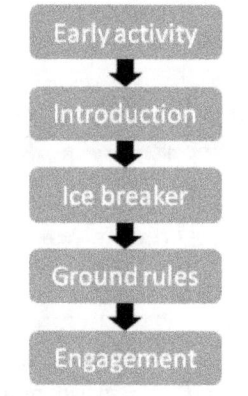

the interface, with the important tools labelled.

- If the participants are not familiar with each other, you could include an ice-breaking exercise. One that works quite well is to display a map and have participants mark their location. You could include further activities that help you to learn more about their backgrounds.

- Present the ground rules, the outcomes and agenda, but don't overdo the detail here, because participants will be keen to get on with things and you probably don't have all day (like you often do in a classroom).

- Now you are into the body of your session. Your first priority is to engage participants and establish the importance and relevance of the topic. A good way to accomplish this is with a series of lead-in questions. These can be implemented using polls or by having participants type answers into the text chat box.

As the session continues, maintain motivation through activities that facilitate social contact. Use job-relevant examples, maintain a brisk pace, and provide frequent opportunities for relevant, meaningful and challenging interactions. Much more on this to follow.

Design a highly-interactive session that takes advantage of the fact that participants are together in real-time. Take particular care to structure the opening of the session, to ensure everyone is relaxed, orientated and raring to go.

You and your co-facilitator can work together as a team however far you are apart geographically

Decide who's doing what

If you have a large group, the topic is complex, the course is new or you are relatively inexperienced as a facilitator, consider working with a second person - a co-facilitator. There are various ways of spreading the load:

- You could 'team teach', dividing up the session into sections and allocating them between you. If you run breakout activities, you could look after different sub-groups.

- Alternatively, have your colleague act as a 'host' or 'producer'. This person is not concerned with the content of the session. Their job is to make sure you can concentrate on your job as a facilitator, by making sure all other aspects of the session runs smoothly. They can keep an eye on everything during delivery, welcomes participants, handled technical questions and problems, respond to messages and manage the chat, launch polls and surveys, set up breakout rooms and shared applications, act as a scribe on the whiteboard, and so on. If you're concerned about the cost of using a second person, then bear in mind that a producer does not need to be an expensive resource.

You don't have to do it all on your own. Consider working with a colleague who can act as a co-facilitator, host or producer.

3

Communicating with voice and live video

3

Communicating with voice and live video

The importance of audio

Audio is likely to be an ever-present in your live session and delivers the vast majority of your content, so for that reason alone it has to be taken seriously as a medium. On top of that, human speech adds a personal element to a session that will activate our inherent social responses. To respect social conventions, we do tend to pay attention when someone is talking directly to us.

It is possible to communicate very successfully using sound as the principle medium, and without eye contact or visible non-verbal behaviour, as demonstrated for many years by radio. With a little care, radio techniques can be applied very successfully to live online sessions. One of the most important techniques is to try and use more than one voice - on radio, the rule of thumb is to limit a single

speaker to 2.5 mins at a time! It also helps to mix voice types and the easiest way to do this is to combine male and female voices. The easiest way to mix up the voices is to have your participants contribute vocally. You might also consider incorporating interviews in your sessions or even pre-recorded audio segments.

It is important to obtain the best possible audio quality, as this can have an effect on how participants perceive the quality of the event as a whole. Make sure you have a reliable broadband connection and use a good quality headset or microphone.

....

Audio plays a major part in any online session. Learn from radio by mixing up the voices as much as possible. Try to make sure your own audio quality is as good as you can get it.

....

Using your voice effectively

The moment you open your mouth you give away something about yourself. This is even more the case when the speaker is heard but not seen. People make assumptions about your mood, levels of stress, general health, place of birth, race, ethnic and genetic build, your education and upbringing, your gender and in some cases even your sexual orientation.

You hear your own voice as a combination of sound from outside your head and sound that's passed along the bones of your skull, which is not how other people hear

Radio techniques can be applied very successfully to live online sessions.

If you are using a free-standing microphone, then don't speak too close to the mic and talk at a normal volume.

it. When you listen to a recording, this is likely to be much closer to how your voice sounds to the outside world, but because it sounds unfamiliar, you may well be shocked when you first hear it.

Linguists and academics use many scientific terms to describe the subtleties of spoken language: tone, idiolect, register, diction, articulation, intonation, projection, pace, pitch, volume, inflection. In essence all a speaker needs to do is decide on the production of the voice (how fast? how loud? how clear? how bright and breezy? how high or low? how deliberate? how earnest?) and about the words themselves (how rhythmical? how formal? how conversational? how 'wordy'?). Don't worry if you have a distinctive national or regional accent. Celebrate your individuality and share it!

The control of your breathing is essential not only for the effective use of a microphone, but also to control nerves. The simplest and easiest exercise is to practise 'dynamic breathing' from your diaphragm. Many of us fall into the habit of very shallow breathing and it is energising as well as good for the control of your voice and nerves when you practise deep breathing.

If you are using a free-standing microphone, rather than a headset, then

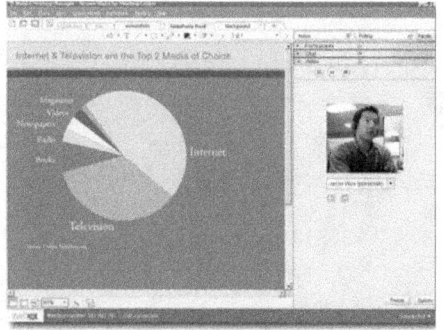

Many web conferencing systems make it possible to provide a live video feed from the facilitator's webcam. Some systems also allow you to show live video feeds of participants.

don't speak too close to the mic - 4-6 inches is close enough. A common mistake is to shout; the whole point of a microphone is to amplify, so speak at a normal volume as if to someone close at hand in the room.

If you're not using video, participants will only have your voice from which to form an opinion about you. Take care to use it effectively.

Using live video

Many web conferencing systems make it possible to provide a live video feed from the facilitator's webcam, which is typically shown in a small window in the virtual classroom interface. Some systems also make it possible to show live video feeds of participants. Live video can make a useful contribution, but using it throughout a session can be very distracting. If you want participants to concentrate their attention on a slide, whiteboard exercise or some

other visual element, then a simultaneous video feed will get in the way.

A short, live video introduction by the facilitator will help to reduce some of the remoteness participants might feel online. But it isn't necessary to continue providing video, because those initial few seconds will create a long-lasting image. Live video can also be useful in question and answer sessions to show the expert as they give their responses.

Look directly into the camera to establish eye contact.

Look directly into the camera to establish eye contact. This may prove quite a strain if you're not a professional TV presenter, which is another good reason for you to keep your use of video to short bursts.

And listening on video can be at least as good as speaking. When participants are talking, use body language, such as eye contacts and nods, to show that you are listening.

It also pays to make sure that you are well lit and that the background shows your working environment as you would want it seen. And don't forget you're on camera! You wouldn't want to be caught picking your nose or worse.

....

Live video can be valuable in short bursts and when you take the trouble to ensure you look professional on camera.

....

4

Communicating using images and text

Communicating using images and text

Why use slides?

Slides are not essential to every virtual classroom session. After all, as we shall see later, you also have the ability to share applications, conduct tours of web sites, carry out whiteboard activities and conduct polls - any of which could act as the primary visual focus. However, slides can be extremely useful both as visual aids and as signposts, as long as they are used properly. Basically that means avoiding the risk of the dreaded 'death by PowerPoint'.

We should not underestimate the power of visuals. Research shows that students learn better from words and pictures than from words alone, which is not surprising when you consider that the majority of our sensory input is visual. Pictures are powerful and they are memorable, as long as you use the right type of picture for the

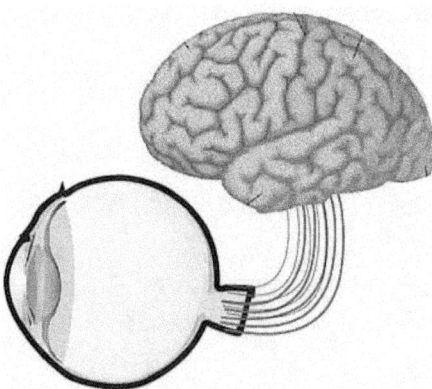

Vision is the predominant sense for acquiring perceptual information.

job. Different types of information require different types of visuals (photos, diagrams, charts, illustrations, etc.) to convey meaning in the clearest possible way.

As Connie Malamed explains in her book *Visual Language for Designers*: "We have no choice but to be drawn to images. Our brains are beautifully wired to the visual experience. For those with intact visual systems, vision is the dominant sense for acquiring perceptual information. We have over one million nerve fibres sending signals from the eyes to the brain, and an estimated 20 billion neurons analysing and integrating visual information at rapid speed. We have a surprisingly large capacity for picture memory, and can remember thousands of images with few errors."

Donald Norman backs this up in his book, *Things That Make Us Smart*: "The power of the unaided mind is highly over-rated. Without external aids, memory, thought and reasoning are all constrained."

....

The majority of sensory input is visual; and in the absence of any other visual focus, slides perform a very useful function.

....

Choosing and using images

Consider the many ways in which images could enhance your session: photos of yourself and other speakers; diagrams to represent processes, principles, structures and layouts; photos to represent actual people, events and objects; photos or

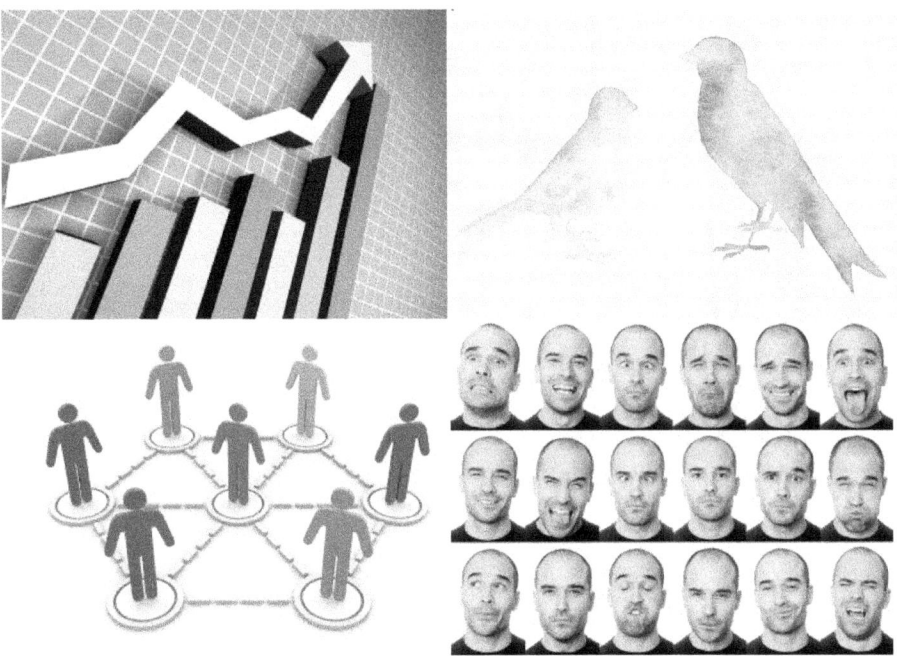

Chartss, illustrations, diagrams and photographs make it possible to describe relationships, trends, structures, likenesses and much more in ways that words can not.

illustrations to represent abstract concepts; screen grabs to show software applications; charts to represent numeric data.

Low-fi graphics, such as simple line drawings, silhouettes and symbols, are often the best solution when learning is your primary goal. If you cut out the visual clutter, you reduce the risk that you'll overload the learner. For maximum clarity, keep the background simple and the colours flat.

Avoid using visuals as mere decoration. As Connie Malamed explains: "A large proportion of visuals in instructional materials serve no useful learning function; they are merely decorative, used in the hope of beautifying the materials or to add interest or humour. But a pig in a suit is still a pig. Don't dress up the pig. Your course doesn't have to look like a video game to be effective."

Animations can be helpful in explaining processes, but they shouldn't be used for effect. They can actually impose an increased mental load on the learner because they convey a great deal of visual information in a transient manner. Elaborate animations are best left for self-paced content.

Lo-fi images are often the best solution when learning is your primary goal, but avoid clip art if you can, because more often than not it looks tired and outdated.

Avoid if you can using the clip-art that comes with PowerPoint and other tools. More often than not, it looks tired and outdated. And if you use stock photography, try to stick to one style of image, so they look good together. If this isn't possible, try applying a common colour tint to each photo (this can accomplished easily in PowerPoint 2007), which makes them look like part of a set. Participants will instinctively follow the gaze of any person in the photo, so it works better when you choose or position images so that people are looking towards the centre of the image or forward, rather than off to the side.

Contrary to popular opinion, you can actually increase interest in the session by using more slides not less - assuming, of course, that the slides contain images and not just text. Rapid slide changes can help to create an environment in which, if you look away, you'll miss something.

If you want your message to be clear, keep your images simple but professional, and make sure they serve a useful purpose.

Position the image so that the gaze of the subject is towards the centre of thes slide or looking forward.

morethanblended.com

Text on slides

Audio is likely to be the primary verbal channel, so don't confuse participants with a second verbal channel in the form of text on the screen. They won't know whether to listen or read; and because they can do the latter much faster than the former, they'll probably end up tuning out what you're saying.

So, use text on slides sparingly. For example:

- For an agenda.

- For titles, which signpost the current topic.

- For anything the participant might want to make a note of, such as terms, URLs, names or quotes.

- For labels on diagrams, photos or charts.

- For lists, bulleted or numbered. Note that when you are presenting items in a list, it is not good practice to show those items that you have yet to cover - reveal these in subsequent slides. And don't be tempted to use your bullets as a script; as an online presenter, if you really need a script you can always have this in front of you in paper format, or in a separate window. Remember to be consistent with the way you phrase each item in a list - if in doubt, read the list out loud and make sure the points sound right together. And be on the lookout for alternatives; look for relationships between points (motion, sequence, parent-child, etc.) that might suggest a more diagrammatic form of display.

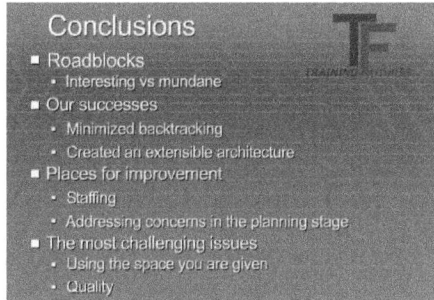

Endless bullet points will only serve to confuse participants ...

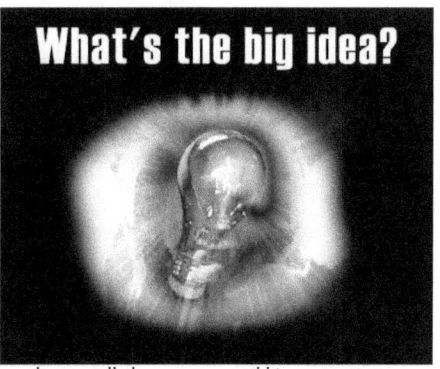

... whereas well-chosen text can add impact to your message.

If you really do need to present a lot of text, distribute this as a separate document, or provide a link to materials that can be read before or after the session.

And remember to keep the text on your slides large enough that it can be seen clearly when viewed in a window rather than full screen.

Your voice will be the primary verbal channel, so don't confuse participants with lots of text on your slides.

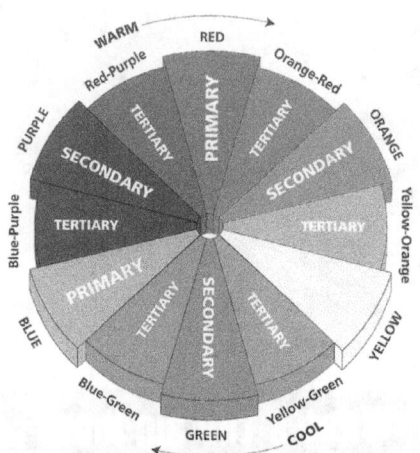

The colour wheel an be used to choose coordinating colours. Each colour on the wheel coordinates with adjacent colours as well as with the colour opposite and its adjacent colours.

Working with colour

Almost a whole library of books has been written on so-called colour theory, so this is a very brief reminder that colour is important. There are four things to bear in mind when you are choosing a colour scheme for presentation online:

1. Colours do not combine in the same way on screen as they do on paper. Graphic designers often use a 'colour wheel' to help them understand which colours work well together on screen. You can find colour wheels on the internet.

2. Indiscriminate use of colour looks horrible. At best it may annoy or distract; at worst it may cause headaches or other discomforts.

3. Colour is a very useful aid to understanding and navigation if it is used thoughtfully. If you use a very limited palette of colours for your basic interface, then contrasting colours can make important information stand out.

4. A proportion of users will suffer some degree of colour-blindness, especially a red-green deficiency.

With colour, less is definitely more. Use a limited palette of colours that work well together on screen and which will not cause problems for those with colour blindness.

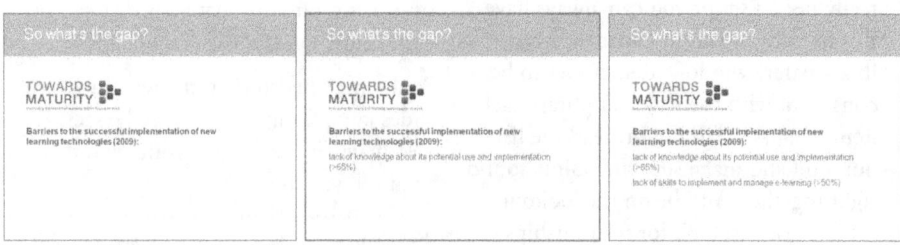

If your slides currently contain builds, you will probably have to rework them as sequences of separate slides. This is relatively easy to achieve if you copy the slide which contains all of the elements and then selectively remove the elemenets you don't need on previous slides.

Re-using slides designed for use face-to-face

Be careful when re-using slides which you normally employ for live presentations. Your slides are likely to be displayed in a smaller window and may degrade in quality when they are converted to the system's own format. The best solution is to keep them simple and bold. You should also be prepared for the possibility that your transitions and animations will not be carried over. That means any builds will have to be displayed as a sequence of individual slides.

If you really do want to preserve your animations, consider using application sharing to present your slides, rather than uploading them to the system's own format. Be aware, though, that with application sharing, the participants' screens are updated only slowly, which means smooth transitions will be impossible.

The slides that you use to present face-to-face may need some adapting for use online.

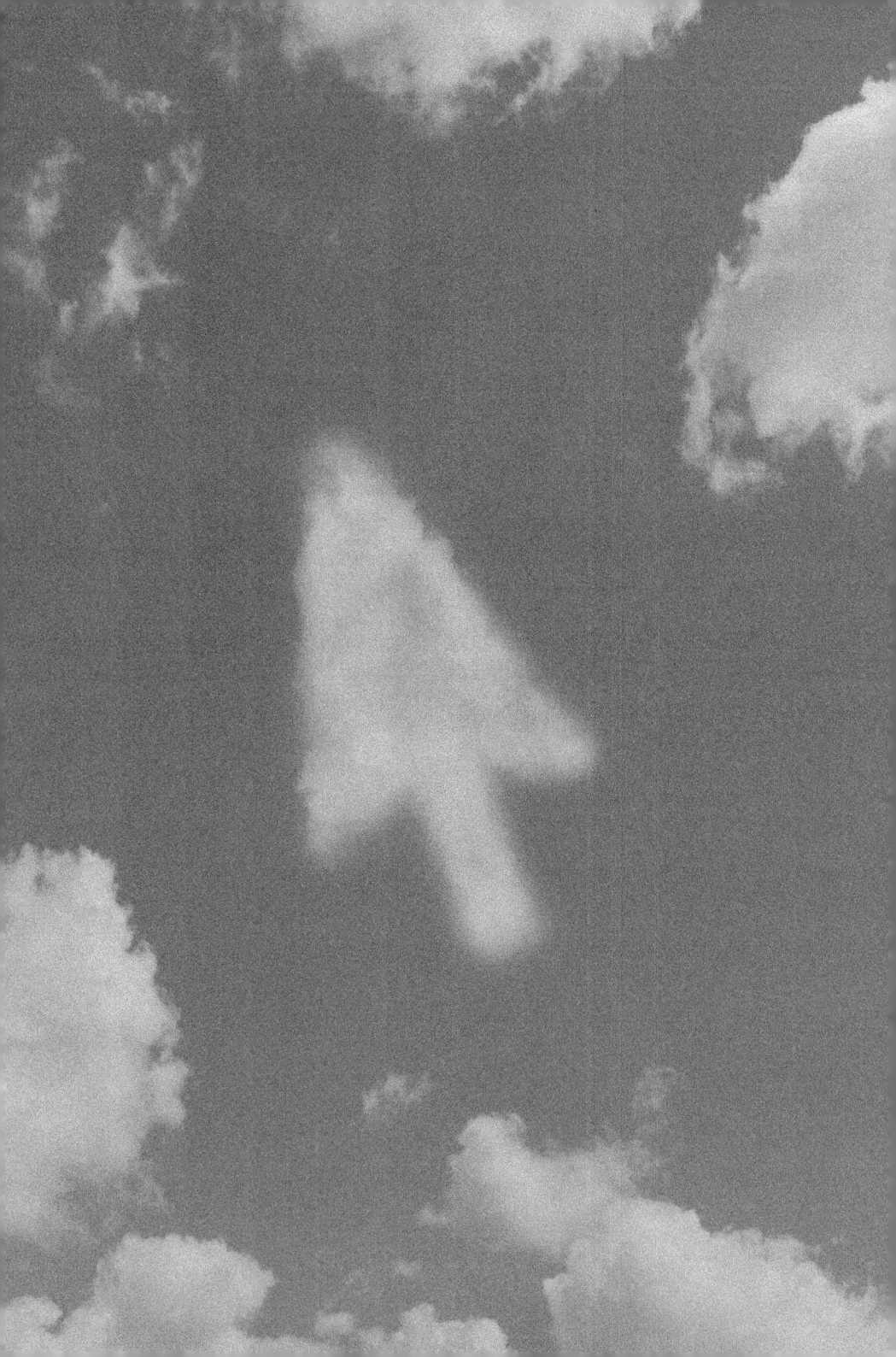

5

Sharing resources

Sharing resources

Application sharing

All web conferencing systems allow the facilitator or any of the participants to share an application on their own desktop. They can also pass control of this application to another participant. This feature has a number of important uses:

- The facilitator can demonstrate how to use a software application and then have participants take turns in using the application. You could create a case study and then pass control from person to person to complete the steps in series. Or you could set up individual breakout rooms in which participants can practise

with the software on their own desktops, getting help from the trainer when needed.

- You can use application sharing as the basis for a role-playing exercise to practise skills that involve technology, e.g. telesales.

- Participants can jointly review a document.

- Presentations can be shared without being uploaded in advance into the web conferencing system's own format. This ensures all the functionality of the original presentation in maintained. This

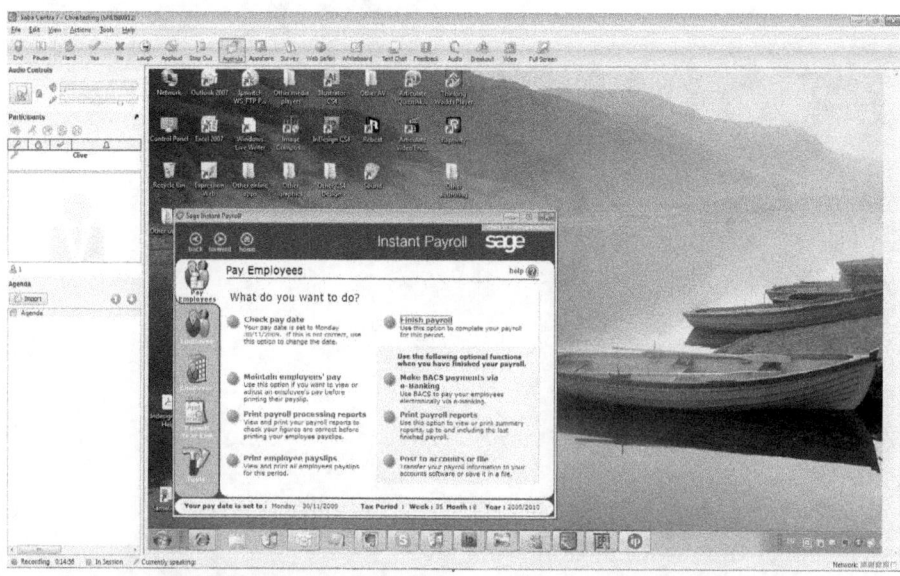

Application sharing allows facilitators to share single applications or, as in this case, a whole desktop.

facility is also useful when the system will only accept PowerPoint upload, whereas you are using an alternative tool such as Keynote or Prezi.

The downside of application sharing is that it demands a fast broadband connection if it is not to appear jerky and disjointed.

Open the application before you need to use it. Get yourself logged in and open any files you need, so you're ready to go.

Find out how much space participants will have on their screens to view applications and then size your window accordingly. This will make sure participants won't have to scroll down or across to see the whole of your application window.

Many systems will also allow you to share your whole desktop, perhaps so you can show how a number of applications work in combination. If this is the case, make sure you close all other applications, especially instant messaging and email - you don't want embarrassing pop-ups to appear while you're presenting!

....

Application sharing is ideal for software demos and for sharing content that can't easily be uploaded onto the system. On the other hand, it can be ponderous without a good broadband connection.

....

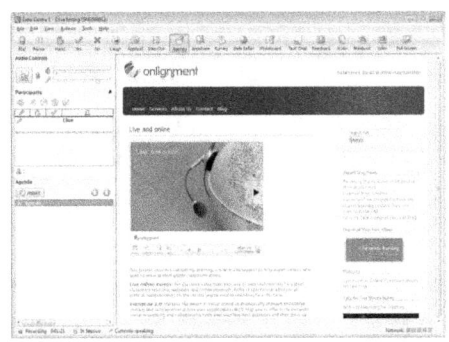

Web tours provide a way for a group to jointly explore a web resoource.

Web tours

Some systems also allow the facilitator to lead participants in exploring a particular web site, whether on the internet or an organisation's intranet. This is useful in that it allows online content to be employed without it being uploaded into the system in advance.

This content could include animations and video, which are not normally available within uploaded slides. It could also include games, quizzes, questionnaires and other activities which participants can then undertake individually.

....

Web tours allow you to show participants round websites and share web content that is not easily uploaded onto the system.

....

6

Building in interactivity

Building in interactivity

Arguments for interactivity

"Consider the worst, most boring college lecture in your life, and remove the cute guy (or girl) down the aisle, and there you have e-learning without interactions. Your students will feel a pressing need to make a grocery list, play Solitaire, or see if their name has an entry yet in Wikipedia. Virtual classrooms only work when instructors employ frequent, relevant interactions." Ann Kwinn, 2007.

Interaction isn't absolutely essential to the learning process. After all, we have probably all learned something useful from what is essentially a 'passive experience' such as reading a book, watching a TV documentary or film, or listening to a radio programme or lecture. You may argue that we supply our own interactivity in these circumstances - taking notes, pondering and reflecting, discussing with others, but there is no formally structured interaction. However, we would probably also agree that externally-mediated interaction, of the sort provided by a teacher, trainer or coach, can certainly help to promote learning: it attracts the learner's attention to ideas that may be relevant; it encourages the learner to work with new ideas, increasing the likelihood that they will be remembered; and it helps the learner to make multiple connections to the new ideas, thereby improving retrieval. Interactivity is very brain-friendly.

But in the virtual classroom, interactivity is doubly important. Here you have an

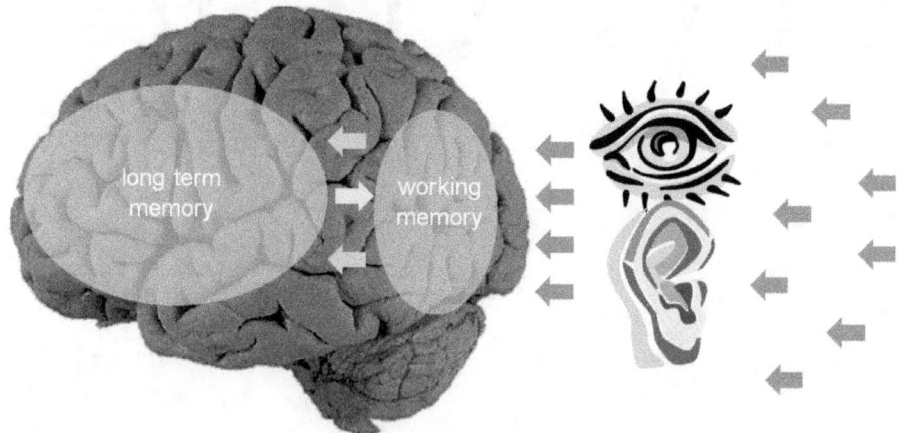

Interaction attracts the learner's attention to relevant new information, bringing it into working memory.; it encourages the learner to work with the new information, helping the transfer to long-term memory; it also helps the learner to make multiple connections to the information, improving the chances of retrieval.

audience that is very easily distracted, by events happening around them, by constant interruptions, and by the easy availability of alternative things to do on their computers. It is also largely an invisible audience - even if each participant is actively engaged, how are you to know? Without regular interactivity, you are flying blind, you are just hoping for the best. Interactivity proves that communication is taking place.

....

Interactivity is brain-friendly. And in the virtual classroom, it provides your only evidence that anything is happening out there.

....

Using text chat

The chat facility typically operates alongside the virtual classroom session, and is available for use at any time. It can be used by participants to answer questions posed by the facilitator, or to ask questions of the facilitator. It can also be used by participants as a 'back channel' for communication between themselves. Some facilitators may find this activity a little strange - after all, we would probably feel uncomfortable if students passed messages to each other during a classroom session. However, many participants find this channel of great use: they exchange contact details, links, thoughts and comments; they help to move the learning process along, without intervention by the facilitator.

Chat is a good option for questions requiring brief, open-ended responses. And

The text chat facility provides an effective 'back channel' for communication between participants, as well as a way of asking and answering questions. Messages can be directed to specific presenters or participants if required. The contents of the chat can also be saved or printed.

if you don't want participants to 'cheat' by just entering the same thing as the last person, ask participants to type in their answers but not press 'send' until told to.

Participants who are more reserved are often more likely to interact when text chat is available. Putting your virtual hand up and speaking through a microphone is a whole lot more intimidating.

If you want students to work in pairs, you don't necessarily need to establish a number of breakout rooms. Rather, you can assign pairings and have participants communicate with each other using the facility in most text chat boxes to direct messages to particular individuals.

Provide time boundaries for chat exercises and be specific about what you are after. To make this clear, type your instructions into the text chat itself or on to the slide (or have a producer or co-trainer do this for you), as well providing them vocally. Remember to allow time for participants to review each other's postings, as they may well have missed these while typing in their own responses.

More often than not, what appears in the chat window will be transitory and disposable. However, if your chat session contains some real gems and you want to keep a permanent record, then use the facility which allows you to save the discussion as a text file when the event is over.

Text chat is a highly flexible and easy-to-use method for maintaining interaction throughout your session.

Using ticks and crosses

Most systems provide a way for facilitators to obtain simple yes/no responses from participants, totalling up the responses automatically. Facilitators can use this mechanism to obtain confirmations ('Can you hear me clearly?', 'Shall I move on?') or to conduct simple polls ('Have you used this system before?', 'Do you have your own blog?').

To get quick responses to simple, closed questions use the tick and crosses.

Using voice interaction

Participant audio is the best option for longer, open-ended responses (or questions) that would require too much typing for the text chat facility. The advantages of are obvious: the communication is more natural and spontaneous, and there is no need for

These buttons on the Saba Centra toolbar allow participants to 'raise their hand's and request the opportunity to interact by voice, and to answer simple binary questions with a yes or no.

typing. However, some moderation is required to avoid everyone speaking at once. Most systems use a 'hands-up' facility, which allows participants to signify that they want to speak. It is then up to the facilitator to 'turn the mic on' or otherwise allow the participant to speak.

Assuming you are using VOIP (internet audio) for sound rather than a teleconference, if participants are to respond by voice, they will need microphones as well as headphones or speakers. This is not a costly problem to solve, because integrated headsets can be obtained for as little as £10.

Voice interaction is best for longer, open-ended responses and questions, but the facilitator needs to moderate the process.

Using the whiteboard

In the context of web conferencing, a whiteboard is a blank screen or a prepared slide, on to which participants can draw or type. Whatever is placed on the whiteboard can be seen by all participants. You can use whiteboards in a wide variety of ways:

- For ice-breaking activities ('Indicate on this map where you are located').

- For capturing expectations at the beginning of a session and then revisiting these at the end.

- For listing participants' ideas, flip chart-style ('In what ways could we use web conferencing?').

- For assessing how things are going ('Draw a picture showing how you're feeling about this topic').

- For structured questions ('What are your objectives for this course?').

- As a place where participants can paste screen shots from an application residing on their computer.

To avoid everyone typing or drawing on top of each other, the facilitator can prepare a slide with sections allocated to each of the participants.

The problem of whiteboard clutter is less of an issue when the system has what is called an 'object-oriented' whiteboard, which allows facilitators or participants to move around any text or other objects which are on the whiteboard after they have been input. An object-oriented approach (which sounds complex, but just means that every object on the whiteboard can be manipulated individually) also makes it easier if you want to run activities where participants place items in sequence or match items with others.

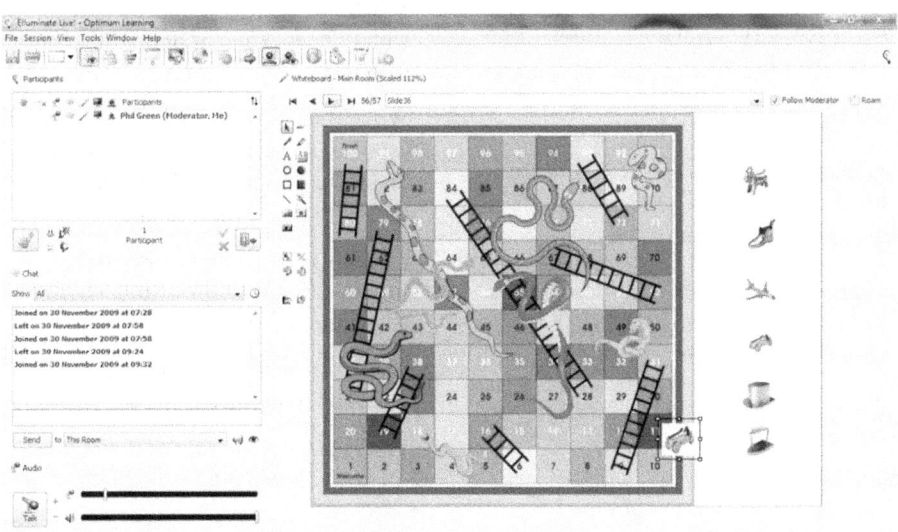

With an object-oriented whiteboard, as shown above in Elluminate, it is possible for each object (graphical element) to be moved independently. This makes it possible to include a wide range of collaborative online games in your sessions, like the snakes and ladders shown here.

Often whiteboards can often be archived for use after the session. If the system won't allow this, just make your own screen grabs.

....

Whiteboards provide plenty of opportunities for imaginative interactions. We're only just beginning to realise what a useful facility they provide.

....

Using polls and quizzes

Polls allow you to ask multiple-choice questions, whether that's to profile participants, survey opinion or check understanding. They are usually set up in advance, although most systems will allow you to modify or add new questions on the fly. An advantage of online polling is that you can obtain totalled-up responses instantly, allowing you to act immediately on the information.

Quizzes and surveys employed during a live session should be brief and advance the cause of the objectives for the session. Otherwise they are better deployed separately, either before or after the session.

....

Use polls and quizzes to survey opinion and check understanding. Keep them quick and ensure they are relevant.

....

Using breakout rooms

Some systems provide you with the facility to allocate participants to groups, have them then undertake activities in those groups within virtual breakout rooms, monitor what is happening in each of

The polling facility allows you to survey opinion or check knowledge. Polls can be created in advance and called up when needed.

these rooms, and then bring the groups back together for a review in plenary. This process mirrors syndicate room activity in a physical classroom and can be used for much the same purposes, for example:

- To run a team competition.

- When you want different groups to work with different content or on different exercises.

- When there are varying levels of expertise in a class, and you want to divide the group into different streams, each with their own facilitator.

- To allow participants to discuss case studies, using their own whiteboards to take notes.

- When you want to conduct a number of role plays in parallel.

With a smaller group of, say, two to five participants, audio can be used more freely than in plenary. If you want, a spokesperson from each group can report to the larger group once everyone has moved back into the main room.

You may need to use a producer or co-trainer to assist with the facilitation. Whichever way you divide responsibilities, it is important for one of the facilitators to drop in regularly to each room to provide guidance. Be aware that participants don't always follow instructions well. When placed into a breakout room, they very often wait for the facilitator to show up to reissue instructions or manage the tools for them. It may pay to set up a template on the whiteboard in each room in advance, to help direct the group.

When participants run into trouble, they need to be able to signal the facilitator to come and help them. This is usually accomplished using private text chat.

Breakout rooms allow learning to occur in parallel in smaller groups, but they will need some looking after.

When to interact

Most experts agree that participants in a virtual classroom should be asked to interact in some way every three to five minutes. It goes without saying that interactivity should not be used for its own sake; each interaction should be meaningful and challenging, and this requires planning and preparation.

Try to involve the whole group in the interaction. Serial participation (one person interacting after another) is rarely the best option as it takes too long. It is better to design activities that can be undertaken in small groups or concurrently, using breakout rooms, chat or the whiteboard.

In *The new virtual classroom* (Pfeiffer, 2007), Ruth Colvin Clark and Ann Kwinn state three universal principles for teaching practical tasks:

> "Participants should be asked to interact every three to five minutes."

- Practical activities should, as far as possible, mirror actual job requirements.

- Practice distributed over time will be more effective than practice which takes place all at one time.

- Start by providing worked examples and then have participants gradually contribute more and more to the process until the exercises become fully-fledged practice assignments.

You may be considering using breakout rooms for group assignments. Clark and Kwinn provide some useful advice about the circumstances in which these are likely to be most effective: when the assignments involve problem-solving tasks, when group sizes are small (3-5), when the assignments are sufficiently complex to benefit from multiple perspectives, and when the assignments and group processes are clearly defined and structured.

Interaction should be regular, but always meaningful. Try to involve the whole group whenever possible.

7

Building up to the session

7

Building up to the session

Putting together a facilitator's guide

There are no hard and fast rules about what should be included in a facilitator guide, but you should consider the following. Whatever format you follow, if there will be more than one person responsible for running the session, make it absolutely clear who is going to be responsible for doing what.

- A brief description of each segment, including the learning objective(s).

- A description of what will be happening visually: a slide, a whiteboard, a video, a web tour, an app share.

- What needs to be said and by whom. Normally you will not need to spell this out word for word, so notes will do.

- What, if anything, needs to be done technically, and by whom, e.g. loading a file or application.

- What, if anything, participants will be required to do. You might list likely or intended responses to help you check that all key points are covered.

- What to do if, for any reason, something doesn't work technically. It's worth having your Plan B thought out in advance.

Create a facilitator's guide to make absolutely clear who does what to whom and when.

Creating any pre and post-session activities and resources

As well as the session itself, you will need to prepare any activities or resources that participants will need before the session, for example: questionnaires; documents to read; videos or podcasts to play; web sites to explore; personal reflection activities, such as goals for the course; self-paced learning materials.

Similarly, you will need to prepare any resources and activities that will be used to follow-up the session, for example: activities using discussion forums; links / further reading; assessments; feedback surveys.

Put together the activities and resources that you intend to use before and after the session.

With any new session, makes sure you rehearse it thoroughly.

Rehearsing

If you're an new facilitator of online sessions, you'd do well to seek out every possible opportunity to be a participant in sessions run by other. You'll learn a great deal by seeing how other facilitators work.

With any new session, and especially if you are a new to online facilitation, run through a rehearsal of your presentation, ideally with an audience of more than one. You don't need to run the session in full; just step through each element in sequence. Make sure you try all the tools and launch all your content and demonstrations at least once, using the same computer that you will be using on the day. Your goal here is to build confidence in using the software with your chosen content and resources and, of course, to make sure that everything works as you expect it to. You may want to record your rehearsal and play it back to see where it could be improved.

Rehearse in as near to life-like conditions as you can make them.

> "Rehearse in as near life-like conditions as you can make them."

Getting yourself prepared

Sort out where you will be delivering the session. Ideally you will be able to use a private, relatively soundproofed room. You might want to prepare a do not disturb sign to hang on the door.

Make a note of the telephone number to call for technical support.

Some facilitators like to have a second computer to hand or a second monitor on their main computer. This can be useful if your web conferencing software lays out the screen differently for facilitators and participants; you can then log in twice and use the second computer or monitor to see what participants are seeing. If you do have a second computer, this can also act as a standby in case you have technical difficulties during the session.

Assuming you are not using a teleconference for audio, then you have choices. Most facilitators use a good quality headset, but you may want to invest in a quality microphone and speakers instead.

If you plan on doing a lot of drawing on the whiteboard, you could buy a small graphics tablet, which allows you to draw much more freely than with a mouse.

If you intend to type large blocks of text into the chat or on to the whiteboard, prepare a document in advance containing all your text. If you have this open during the session, you can easily copy and paste the text in when you need it. Print hard copies of any text you intend to read, as you'll find it easier than reading from the screen.

Make sure your hardware is up to the job and that you have all your materials to hand.

Briefing participants

Before the session, contact all your participants to explain the logistics for the session, including start and end times, an overview of what you will be doing during the session, details about you, instructions for any pre-work assignments and contact information. Some facilitators even recommend calling participants beforehand by telephone to help establish an effective personal relationship between you.

You might also prepare a guide which participants can print out and consult throughout the session, including instructions for the activities that they will be asked to perform. However, it should not replicate your slides, because you want their attention to be focused on the screen, not the handout.

Many participants believe that anything really important will be covered in the live event and that pre-work is therefore unnecessary. If you continue to support this notion by spending time playing catch-up with those who have not done the pre-work, then this situation will persist. Make absolutely clear in your instructions that the pre-work is an essential component of the course and that you will not be spending time covering it in the live sessions.

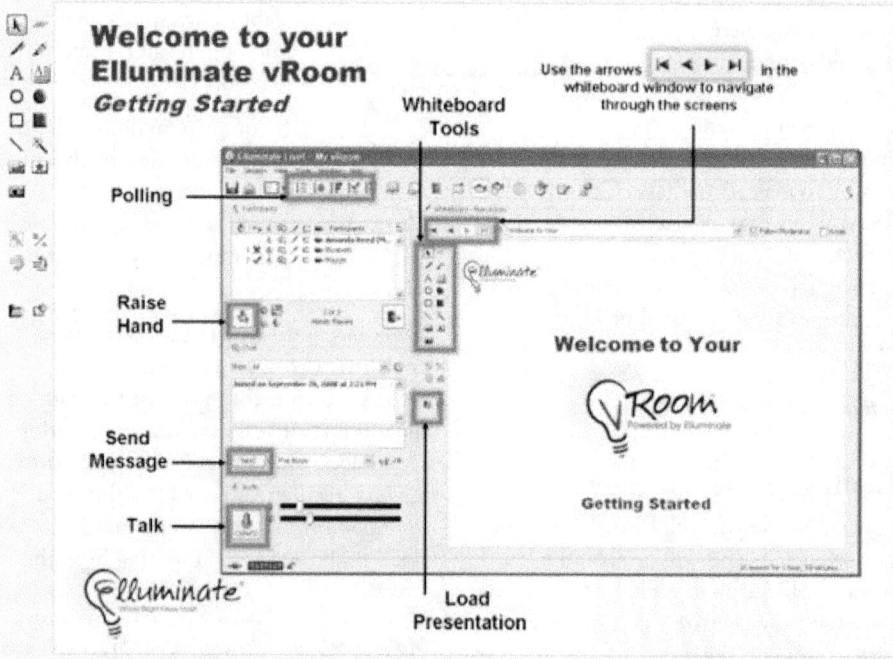

Graphics like these can be used to help familiarise participants with the system before the commencement of the session.

morethanblended.com

Make sure participants have all the information they need to join the session and to engage in it successfully. Emphasise that pre-work is just that.

Familiarising participants with the system

You have a number of options for ways in which to induct participants into use of the web conferencing software:

- Prepare a guide that provides all the instructions necessary for participants to use the web conferencing tool effectively. This could be a one-pager that they could print and keep by them while they attend the session, or a more lengthy document that they can view online.

- Ask participants to log in up to 15 minutes early so you can handle any technical problems before the session begins.

- Conduct a short tutorial before the session.

- Create a short video or Flash animation that can run before the session starts.

- If your participants are new to live online learning but will be participating in a number of online sessions, then you could consider running a special 'learning to learn online' course. If you will only be running live sessions, then this could be a single session prior to the commencement of the course. If the course is a blended solution, using synchronous and asynchronous elements, then your 'learning to learn online' should include use of all the key elements of the blend.

Participants who are new to your web conferencing tool will need some help to find their way around. There are plenty of ways of doing this.

8

Facilitating the session

8

Facilitating the session

Final preparations

It's a good idea to log in at least a few days before the session to make sure everything works. On the day itself, take some time to prepare your physical environment:

- Log on nice and early.

- Turn off anything that could make a noise, including telephones and fax machines. Muzzle the dog! If you have no choice but to run the session in an open office, then explain to your colleagues what you will be doing and ask them to keep their voices low.

- Have a pen and notepad to hand to jot down reminders, observations and actions for follow up.

- You may only be online for an hour or so, but it's still useful to find a comfortable chair, dress in layers and keep adequate supplies of water to hand (avoid coffee because this will only encourage you to speak more quickly - a problem that will already have been exacerbated by the rush of adrenaline you'll have experienced when you started the session). Hopefully you won't be doing all the talking, but you might still like to have some throat lozenges handy (but take them out before you speak!).

- Close un-needed applications.

....

Log-in early and then get yourself completely prepared, ready to welcome participants.

....

Welcome participants warmly as they arrive.

Welcoming participants

Welcome participants warmly as they arrive. They'll appreciate it. You might also encourage participants to welcome each other - text chat is ideal for this. It pays to encourage facilitative practices from everyone, not just the facilitator.

Show participants where to find the important buttons, including the laughter, applause, agree and disagree icons, and encourage their use. Give everyone a chance to try them out and use them often yourself. As Jonathan Finkelstein explains in *Learning in Real Time*, "There isn't a constructive criticism so harsh that it cannot be softened by a ;-) or a student response so good that it cannot be followed by enough :-) :-). And guilt, an instructor's secret weapon in boosting many students' motivation, is often well-served by a strategically placed :(emoticon."

Ask participants to use the 'stepped away' button (or similar, depending on your system) when they have to leave the computer or shift their attention, and then step back in when they are back on board again.

If you are using teleconferencing for audio, then suggest everyone is off mute - this will create an expectation for interaction.

Provide a warm welcome to every participant as they arrive. Make sure they know how to use the most important tools.

Dealing with multitasking

With online sessions generally, it's a safe assumption that some participants will be multitasking - checking emails, answering the phone, listening to music, finishing off a report, and so on - how ever well your session has been put together and run.

In a virtual classroom, multitasking will be less common than with a webinar or an online meeting, but will still occur to some extent. Participants just can't help themselves - the distractions are so persistent and so inviting. One way you could attempt to address this is to start the meeting by asking each participant to identify and then remove a possible distraction.

Most systems have annotation tools available to the trainer, such as pointers, markers, drawing tools and so on. Use these to direct attention to particular aspects of your slides. And, because their use is a form of movement, this will attract the attention of anyone who is losing focus.

According to Kevin Kelly of *Wired* magazine, "The only factor becoming scarce in a world of abundance is human attention." Learners have no trouble staying interested in things that they find relevant or fun. What they don't want is to hear someone talk for hours on end.

Multitasking is inevitable but a well designed and executed session will keep this to a minimum.

It's a safe assumption that some of your participants will be doing their email.

Mute your microphone when you ask a question. This may be the only chance you get to catch your breath and have some water.

Asking questions

Once you have asked a question and given instructions on how to answer, mute your own microphone. These will be the only times available for you to have some water, sort out your papers, clear your throat, and generally get your breath back. In addition, if you stay quiet, you encourage participants to pay attention to what's happening on the screen.

Don't be afraid of a little silence after you've asked a question. Give participants time to gather their thoughts and respond before you move on. Some participants will be new to the technology, and it may take them a while to figure out how to raise their hand or how to respond in the chat area.

When you've asked a question, take a breather. Give participants plenty of time to respond.

Taking questions

When students raise their hands, send chat messages, or provide other forms of feedback, you need to be aware of this and prepared to react. Don't let questions and comments go without acknowledgement for long.

If you are working with a co-facilitator, this person can take responsibility for scanning the text chat and the participant list for questions coming in. If they feel there is a question you should address straight away, they can alert you by sending you a private text message.

Don't take a complicated question in the middle of getting your point across. You - or your co-facilitator - might like to set up a 'parking lot' to hold complex or unrelated questions for dealing with later. This could take the form of a specially-prepared whiteboard or just a list on a piece of paper.

Be alert for questions. Park questions that are off topic for later.

Maintain a 'parking lot' for complex or off-topic questions.

Timekeeping

Schedule more time than you think you will need and then plan to end on or before when the schedule says.

Don't hold everyone else up while you get latecomers up-to-speed and don't spend twenty minutes asking everyone to introduce themselves - in an online session, none of you has time for this.

....

An online session is short so don't waste time. Try to ensure you finish on or before the scheduled end time.

....

9

Following up

9

Following up

Take aways and follow ups

Your handouts only need to cover the main points of your session, because the recording is always available for those who want to recap on the detail. You can supplement this with step-by-step procedure guides, checklists, templates and other job aids, as well as links to additional resources. Avoid the temptation to use your presentation slides as a handout, because slides that include enough detail to stand-alone are unlikely to make good visual aids.

All major web conferencing systems allow you to make a recording of a live online session as a resource for those participants who want to go back and review the session, or as an aid for those who were not able to attend at the scheduled time. Ideally the playback software provided with the system will allow viewers to fast forward past the bits that are less interesting to them. Some will also allow the recording to be edited so that the viewer can skip directly to particular points, such as the start of a new topic or activity. Depending on the system, you might be able to edit the recording to remove any sections which would obviously be of no interest to someone who wasn't at the event - in particular if there were any technical difficulties.

If the text chat is not included in the recording, a transcript can usually be saved separately as a simple text file.

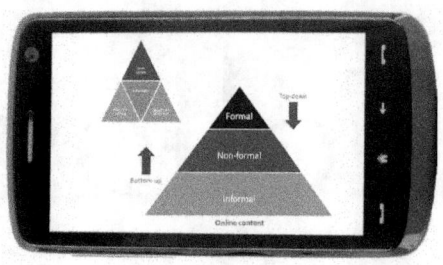

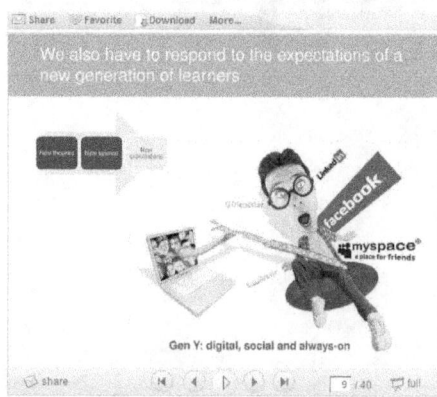

Presentations can be adapted to act as stand-alone resources in a number of ways. Pictured above are examples of an Articulate presentation, a slide show running as a movie on a mobile phone, and a presentation on SlideShare.

If your session incorporates a slide presentation which you want participants to be able to refer back to at a later date, you have a number of options other than just making a live recording of the session:

- You could use a PowerPoint add-in like Articulate or Adobe Presenter to add a narration to the slides and convert the output to Flash for deployment online.

- You could also add a narration and convert the presentation to video using a tool like Camtasia. The video can then be made available online for playback on PCs or through mobile devices, such as iPods and smart phones.

- Another alternative is to add some text to the slides so that they become self-explanatory, then share them as a PowerPoint file or on the SlideShare website.

Provide opportunities for reflection and/or discussion immediately following the session, perhaps using an asynchronous medium, such as a forum. If you want to get the discussion going, end your session with a challenge or a question to be tackled using the forum. Take an active role in the forum yourself, responding to questions and contributing to the discussions, without attempting to dominate the process.

Decide what you want to leave participants as reference, whether that's a handout, a recording or a re-packaged version of your presentation. Consider using a forum or some similar tool to allow participants to continue reflecting on the session content.

Evaluating the session

To evaluate the session effectively, you need to return to your goals for conducting the session in the first place and see how you have fared. Your effectiveness in meeting your goals can be examined at a number of different levels:

> "You'll want to evaluate your session in terms of both its effectiveness in meeting your learning and performance goals and its efficiency."

- Did you obtain a positive response to the session from participants? This might seem like an unimportant issue but it is not, because positive reactions are important in attracting future participants. It's particularly important to find out if there is any negative feeling, because bad news travels much faster than good.

Don't give yourself a hard time if you receive bad feedback; a complaint is an opportunity to win a customer for life - you just have to handle it effectively. Be a good listener and try not to be defensive. Be clear about what action you are going to take, if any, and then make sure you carry it out. You'll be able to assess reactions to some extent through your observations of participants as the session progresses. You can also measure the response more formally using some form of questionnaire. Most web conferencing systems have the capability to deliver questionnaires, although if you want something more comprehensive, you'd be better off pointing participants to a separate tool as an activity to be completed later.

With an important new project, you may want to have more informal discussions with participants as you test out the programme at various stages of development.

- You will also want to return to your learning objectives, to see whether these have been achieved. You may be able to get the confirmation you need by activities conducted within the session - quizzes, role-plays, case studies, etc. Other times, the learning objectives can only be effectively measured through some activity that occurs subsequent to the session, such as a practical project or assignment.

- You can go further to assess the level to which the new learning has been put into practice and whether this has had a positive effect on the organisation's performance. Evaluation at these higher levels is important but not in any way particular to live online learning, so we won't be examining them in any detail here.

Your use of live online learning is likely to be influenced as much by the potential efficiencies of the medium as it is by its effectiveness in achieving learning and performance goals. There are several ways in which you can measure efficiency:

- Bums on seats: This is a measure not only of the popularity of your offering, but also the extent to which you are utilising capacity. If your sessions are half-empty, you are wasting trainer time. If you regularly have to cancel sessions and reschedule, then you are inconveniencing your participants.

- Cost: Online sessions are likely to yield major cost benefits when compared to face-to-face alternatives. Don't forget to look at all the savings, both direct (money that has to be paid out, such as for travel and subsistence) and indirect (overheads that can be applied elsewhere, such as staff costs).

- Time: Sometimes it seems that time is more scarce than money. Online sessions save a considerable amount of time that

Evaluating effectiveness	Evaluating efficiency
Participant reactions	Take-up
Achievement of learning objectives	Use of capacity
	Cost
Changes in behaviour	Duration
	Timeliness
Impact on business metrics	Environmental impact

Evaluating effectiveness and efficiency

morethanblended.com

would otherwise be spent travelling. They can also be implemented in a more timely fashion, without so much advance notice.

- Environmental benefits: By reducing or even eliminating the need to travel for training, you could see a dramatic reduction in your organisation's carbon emissions. Use tools such as Learning Footprint to calculate the environmental benefits of this approach.

....

You'll want to evaluate your session in terms of both its effectiveness in meeting your learning and performance goals and its efficiency.

....

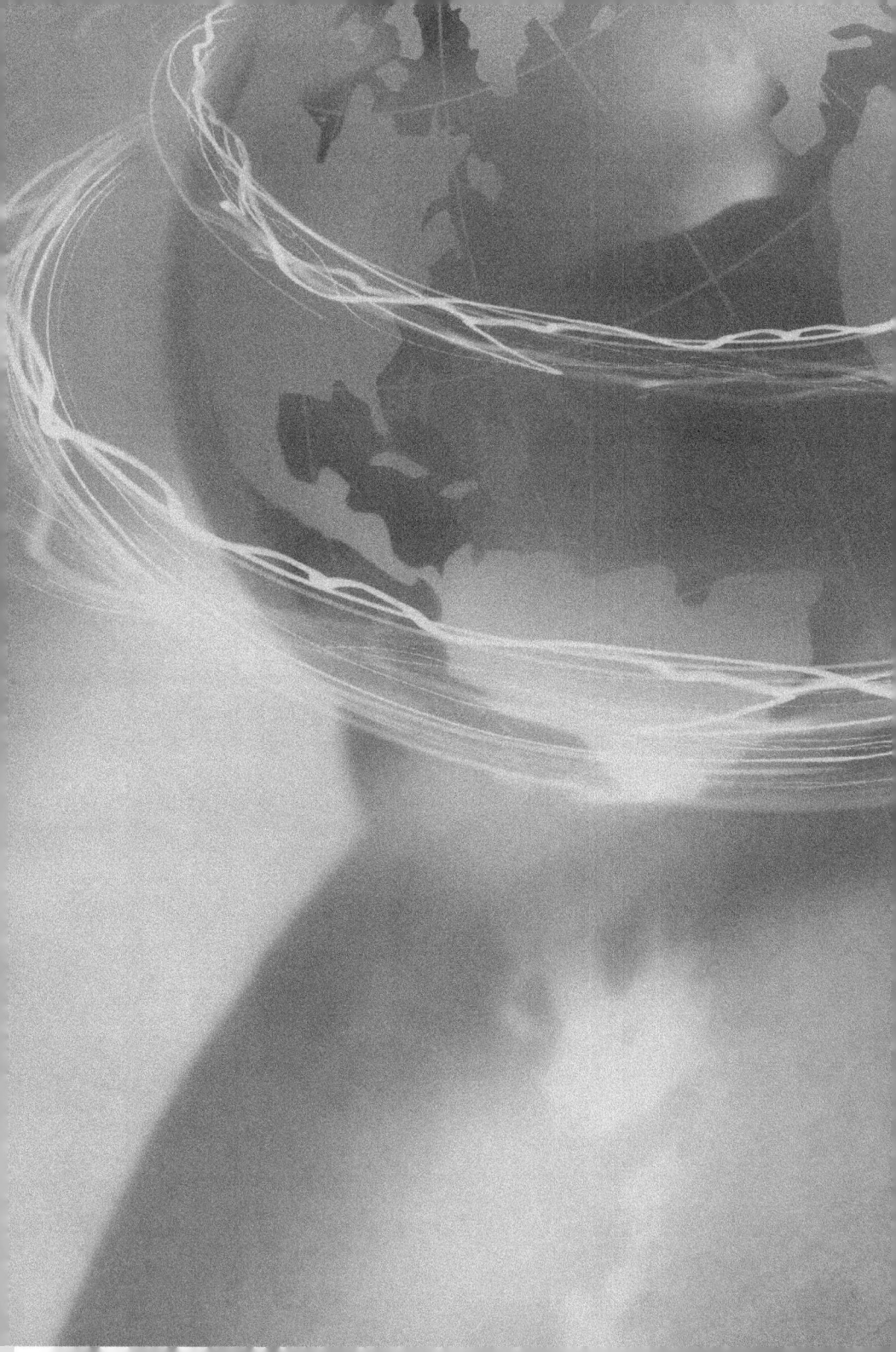